FASHION LOOK

A DESIGN & ILLUSTRATION COLLECTION

柳沢元子 著

ファッションデザイナーが描くモードイラストレーション

FASHION LOOK

DESIGN & ILLUSTRATION COLLECTION

Motoko Yanagisawa

g

Graphic-sha

装丁・レイアウト・写真 ： 貴 田 庄
Book Design Layout Photography ： Sho Kida

FASHION LOOK
A DESIGN & ILLUSTRATION COLLECTION

by Motoko Yanagisawa ©

Copyright © 1992 by Graphic-sha Publishing Co., Ltd.
1-9-12, Kudan-kita, Chiyoda-ku Tokyo 102 Japan

ISBN4-7661-0671-7

First published in March 25th 1992
Translation by Leslie Harrington

Printed in Japan by Kinmei Printing Co., Ltd.

プロローグ

Prologue

ファッション画にはデザイナー自身が描いたものと，イラストレーターが描いたものの2種類があります。

しかし，雑誌や広告では，どちらかというとイラストレーターの描いたファッション画を目にすることが多いと思います。デザイナーは自分ではファッション画を描かないのでしょうか。

ファッション画は，デザイナー自身が描くことが理想です。自分の頭の中に浮かんだ服のイメージを，他の人が紙のうえに完全に移しかえることは不可能なことです。

また，ファッション画を描かないデザイナーは，創作することの楽しみを知らない人といえます。なにかをデザインすることは，まず白い紙に線を描き，色をつけて，試行錯誤することから始まるのではないでしょうか。無から有への苦しみを経験せずに，優れたデザイナーになることはありえません。このことは，ファッションデザイナーだけではなく，他のクリエイティヴな仕事をする人にもあてはまるでしょう。

魅力的なファッション画を描くことは難しいことではありません。この本では，顔の描き方や線画からはじめ，テキスタイル，毛皮，ニット，インナー，アウター，子供，メンズ，靴や靴下など，ファッション企画に必要なさまざまなアイテムを採りあげています。そして，筆，色鉛筆，水彩絵具，パステル，マーカーの使い方を説明し，どのように描き，着色するかを具体的に紹介しています。服のデザインをいかすファッション画の描き方がよく理解できるでしょう。

ファッションを専門とする人，学校でファッションを学んでいる人だけではなく，広く，イラストレーションにたずさわっている人にも興味を持てるようになっています。本書を参考に，思い通りのファッション画を描けるデザイナーをめざして下さい。

Fashion sketches may either be drawn by designers or illustrators. However, it is more common to see illustrations drawn by the latter in magazines and advertisements. Does this mean that designers do not draw their own illustrations？

It would be best to have designers draw their own fashion illustrations. It is impossible for a third party to accurately convey on paper someone else's image of a design. It can also be said that designers who do not draw their own illustrations do not understand the fun of creating something. Designing something should start with drawing lines on a blank piece of paper, coloring the sketch, and creating a design through trial and error. It is not possible to become a skilled designer without first experiencing the difficulties of creating something from nothing. This applies not only to fashion designers, but to those in other creative fields, as well.

It is not difficult to draw attractive fashion illustrations. This book will teach you to draw all of the necessary items in fashion illustrations, including faces, line sketches, different textiles, fur, knits, inner and outer wear, children's and men's clothes, shoes, and socks. We will also explain how to use brushes, colored pencils, water colors, pastels, and various markers. Specific examples will be discussed to explain how to use these to color the sketches. By studying these examples, you should be able to fully comprehend how to draw fashion illustrations that will bring out the unique characteristics of the design.

We have created a book that is interesting to all people involved in the illustration fields, and not only to those specializing in fashion or studying it in school. We hope that you will use this book as a reference and aim at becoming a designer capable of drawing all desired fashion illustrations.

目　次・CONTENTS

線画

ファッション画の基本は線にあります。ファッション画を魅力的なものにするためには，自分の好みにあった線を見つける必要があります。さまざまな用具がありますから，どんなものを使えば求める線が描けるか確かめてください。ここでは筆ペン，フェルトペン，鉛筆，ペン，ロットリングの5種類の用具で線について考えてみます。

筆ペンは強弱がつけやすく，生き生きとした勢いのよい線を描くことができます。手早く動かし，2度書きが難しいので，慣れるまで少し時間がかかるでしょう。

フェルトペンは平均的な太さで，安定した線を描くことができます。水性と油性がありますが，あとで着色する時は油性のフェルトペンを使います。

鉛筆はソフトな調子が表現でき，線を重ねることもできますが，線の濃さが不十分なので，どちらかというと下絵的なファッション画となります。

ペンも強弱をつけやすく，細く硬い線が得られますが，曲線を描く時に線が不安定になるので注意しましょう。

ロットリングの場合は同じ太さの線で描けますが，そのために線が一定しすぎて，魅力のないファッション画になる時があります。

これらの用具のほかにも，色々なものがありますから自分の個性を出せるものを見つけてください。この時，ファッション画を描く紙質も考慮してください。例えば，ロットリングは軟らかすぎる紙にはあいません。紙質によっては用具の特徴をよく引きだせない時もあります。ファッション界では着色のしない線だけの絵がよく用いられます。パタンナーがこれらのファッション画を見て，立体に形をおこしてゆくわけです。そのために線画であっても，魅力的なものにする必要があります。と同時に，服としてデザインの意図がよく読み取れるように，明確に描くことを心がけましょう。

Line Drawings

The basis of a fashion illustration lies in the line. In order to create an attractive fashion illustration, it is first necessary to find a line that suits your tastes. Since there are a variety of tools available, determine which will produce the desired effect. We will discuss the following five tools here: brush pen, felt-tipped pen, pencil, pen, and rotring.

With a brush pen it is possible to alter the intensity, stressing particular areas, creating lively lines. It is necessary to use quick strokes, and since it is difficult to draw over the first lines, practice is necessary to master the technique.
Felt-tipped pens are used to draw stable lines of equal thickness. There are water-and oil-based pens. If color will be applied later, select an oil-based type.
Although pencils produce soft expressions, and can be used to apply several lines over each other, the results are often too light and weak. A fashion illustration using a pencil becomes more of a rough sketch.
Pens are useful for varying the intensity, as well, and result in thin, hard lines. Remember, however, that the lines become unstable when drawing curves.
When rotring are used the thickness of lines is quite equal, but this often results in fashion illustrations that are unattractive, because of the lack of variety in the lines.

There are many other tools that may be used, so you should find one that is the most suitable for your purpose.
When doing so, consider the paper that is to be used, as well. For example, rotring is not suitable for soft paper. Depending on the quality of paper, you may not be able to take advantage of the characteristics of the particular tool being used. In the world of fashion you will find that sketches of lines only, without color, are often used. A pattern specialist looks at these illustrations and creates a three-dimensional shape. Even if the purpose is simply to do this, it is necessary to make the line drawing attractive. At the same time, it must also be accurate, so that the purpose of the design, resulting in clothes, is made clear.

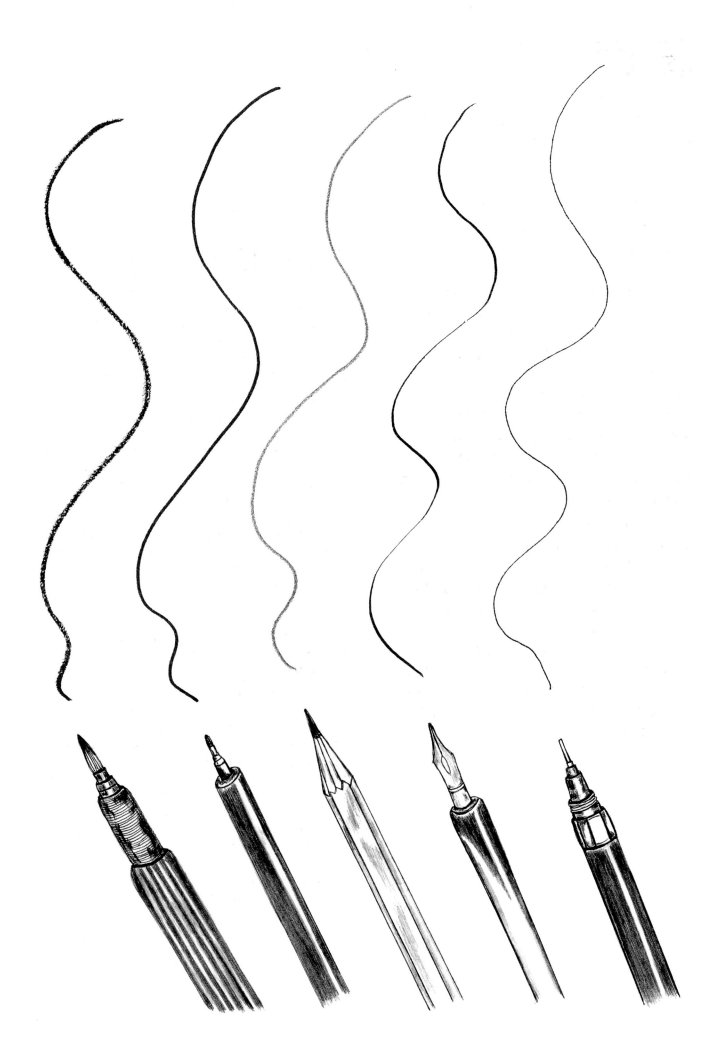

筆ペン
Brush pen

フェルトペン
Felt-tipped pen

鉛筆
Pencil

ペン
Pen

ロットリング
Rotring

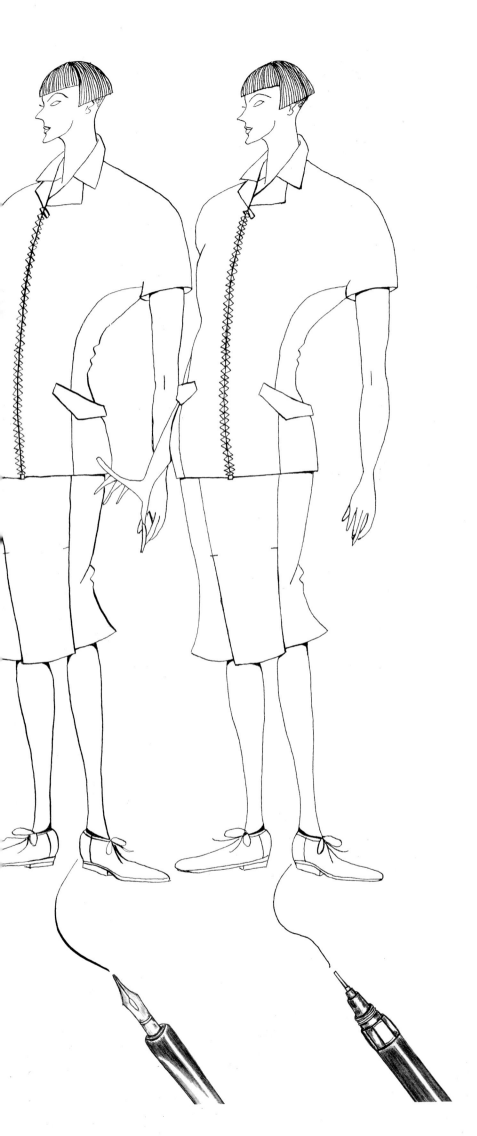

筆ペン
強弱のある生き生きとした線

フェルトペン
平均的な安定した線

鉛筆
ソフトな調子の線

ペン
強弱のある細く硬い線

ロットリング
細くて硬い一定な線

Brush pen
A lively line showing
a variety in intensity.

Felt-tipped pen
An average, stable line.

Pencil
A soft line.

Pen
A thin, hard line showing
a variety in intensity.

Rotring
An even, thin, and hard line.

顔

ファッション画では，洋服のデザインについ目がゆきがちですが，人物を描いている以上，顔は重要な役割を果たします。魅力的な顔が描ければ，ファッション画としても成功していることでしょう。というのは，顔の流行はきわめて時代に左右されているからです。メーキャップやヘアースタイルなどが，どんなに流行に敏感か経験しているのではないでしょうか。

顔の描き方のポイントを述べましょう。

ひとりひとりの個性が違うように，人の顔にもさまざまあります。そこでまず，自分の好きな顔立ちや描きたいヘアースタイルを知る必要があります。顔の向きには，横向き，斜め向き，正面向きなどがありますが，色々な向きの顔を描けるようになって下さい。表情は目を上げて描けば描くほど主張のある顔に，目を下げて描けば描くほどやさしくおだやかな顔になります。ヘアースタイルは顔を描く時に大きな役割を果たします。ヘアースタイルにもはっきりとした流行があり，服のデザインと切り離しては考えられないものなので，雑誌などを参考に，よくヘアースタイルを研究して下さい。

Faces

When drawing fashion illustrations it is easy to concentrate only on the design of the clothes. It is necessary, however, to remember that the face plays a very important role in the illustration. The illustration will be a success if an attractive face is drawn. This is because the trend of faces is greatly influenced by the times. You are no doubt aware how sensitive make-up techniques and hair styles are to current trends.

As with individual characteristics, human faces are also unique. It is, therefore, necessary to first determine the features and hair styles that you wish to portray.

Practice drawing views from the front and side, as well as from other angles. The face becomes more assertive when the eyes are looking up, and more peaceful and kind the more they are looking down. The hair style plays an important role in drawing a face. There are definite trends in hair styles, and it is not possible to think of them apart from the garment's design. Use magazines and other forms of media to study different hair styles.

Gouache, Pastel, Hahnemühle paper

Gouache, Pastel, Hahnemühle paper

Gouache, Pastel, Hahnemühle paper

Gouache, Pastel, Hahnemühle paper

Gouache, Pastel, Hahnemühle paper

Gouache, Pastel, Hahnemühle paper

テキスタイル

テキスタイルには無地ものと柄もの（プリント）があります。ファッション企画では，無地ものの使われる割合が大きいのに対して，柄ものは流行によって使われる量が多くなったり少なくなったりします。

ブランドのイメージやターゲットを，柄ものを使うことで強めることができます。また，そのシーズンのテーマを伝えるためには柄ものは大きな役割を果たします。しかし，柄は無地より個性が強く，記憶に残るため，次のシーズンでは同じものを使うことができません。

ここではプリントのイメージ作りと完成したプリントを数点紹介しています。さらにそのプリントを使ったファッション画に絵具を使い，プリントがよくはえるように，濃いめにぬったり，薄めにぬったりして表現しています。

Textiles

There are plain and printed textiles. Fashion designs often use plain textiles, and the volume of printed ones varies according to the current trends.

It is possible to stress the brand's image and target through the use of printed textiles. This type of textile also plays a large role in conveying the season's theme. However, since prints have more character than plain cloth, leaving a more definite impression on the viewer, it is not possible to use the same textile the following season.

We have selected a few printed textiles here, discussing how to create a print's image. Actual fashion illustrations have been introduced as well, using thick and thin paint to bring out the characteristics of the pattern.

Gouache, Pastel, Bresdin Japon paper

濃いめぬり

水をあまりまぜない絵具で全体をぬる。地色が完全に乾いてから，次の色をのせてゆく。

Thick Paint

Paint the entire illustration using a paint with little water. Apply the next color once the base color is completely dry.

Gouache, Pastel, Bresdin Japon paper

薄めぬり

水を多く混ぜた絵具をぬる。むらになりやすいので，手早く筆を使うことが大切。

Thin Paint

Use paint with a lot of water. Since thin paint becomes uneven quite easily, it is necessary to apply the color quickly.

Gouache, Pastel, Bresdin Japon paper

花よりのイメージ

プリントの中で花の模様は一番多く使われます。リバテ
ィプリントのような小さな花柄から大きな花柄のプリン
トまで，また，リアルに描いたものから抽象的に描いた
ものまでさまざまあります。ここではチューリップをモ
チーフに，比較的リアルに描いた模様で，プリントをデ
ザインしてみました。

Floral Images

Floral images are the most common patterns used on
printed textiles. There are small prints such as those used
by Liberty, large prints, realistic patterns, and abstract
ones. We have designed a fabric here using tulips as the
motif, with the pattern drawn relatively realistically.

40×40 cm

文字よりのイメージ

日常生活で使われている文字の中から，ここではアルファベットを選び，プリントにデザインしています。文字にもさまざまなものがありますが，その中でもアルファベットはよくモチーフに選ばれます。書体によってもできたプリントがかなり異なってくるので，文字の形に注意して下さい。

Character Images

We have chosen the alphabet, from characters used in our daily lives, to design the fabric. Although there are many characters available, the alphabet is most commonly chosen as the motif. Pay attention to the variations of typeface, since the shape and style of characters will greatly change the image of the print.

日常生活で使われている文字の中から，ここではアルファベットを選び，プリントにデザインしています。文字にもさまざまなものがありますが，その中でもアルファベットはよくモチーフに選ばれます。書体によってもできたプリントがかなり異なってくるので，文字の形に注意して下さい。

日常生活で使われている文字の中から，ここではアルファベットを選び，プリントにデザインしています。文字にもさまざまなものがありますが，その中でもアルファベットはよくモチーフに選ばれます。書体によってもできたプリントがかなり異なってくるので，文字の形に注意して下さい。

30×25 cm

葉よりのイメージ

自然の中にある葉をモチーフに採りあげました。葉も花
と同様に，プリントに多く使われる図案のひとつです。
このプリントにもリアルなものから抽象的にデザインし
たものまであります。ここでは小さなプリントと大きな
プリントをデザインしています。

Leaf Motifs

We have selected leaves from nature as the motif.
Leaves, as with flowers, are often used as the motif
for printed textile. The designs may be realistic or
abstract. We have designed large and small leaves
here.

葉よりのイメージ

自然の中にある葉をモチーフに採りあげました。葉も花
と同様に，プリントに多く使われる図案のひとつです。
このプリントにもリアルなものから抽象的にデザインし
たものまであります。ここでは小さなプリントと大きな
プリントをデザインしています。

Leaf Motifs

We have selected leaves from nature as the motif.
Leaves, as with flowers, are often used as the motif
for printed textile. The designs may be realistic or
abstract. We have designed large and small leaves
here.

24×24 cm

15×15 cm

抽象模様 Abstract patterns

30×30 cm

このテキスタイルは黄，赤，青の
三色の油絵具を用いて作っていま
す。筆ではなく，ローラーに絵具
をつけ，回転させながら描きます。

This textile has been colored
using yellow, red, and blue oil
paints. Rather than using a
brush, the paint is applied to a
roller. Color by rotating the
roller.

Gouache, Pastel, Bresdin Japon paper

幾何学模様　Geometric patterns

24×24 cm

15×15 cm

Gouache, Pastel, Bresdin Japon paper

毛皮と革

しばらく前から，自然保護，動物保護などが社会的な問題になっています。そして本物の動物の毛皮を積極的に使うデザイナーが少なくなっています。そんな社会の動きに合わせ，かってはあまり好まれなかったイミテーションの毛皮（フェイクファー）が多く使われるようになっています。

さらに最近は，本物にもっと近いイミテーション毛皮が開発され，デザイナーは本物とイミテーションをうまく使いわけるようになっています。またイミテーションは，ナチュラル中心の色だけでなく，さまざまな色に自由に染めることができ，本物とくらべ価格も安いので，ファッションの企画に抵抗なく使われるようになりました。ここでは本物の毛皮でも，イミテーションの毛皮でも利用できるファッション画を描いています。さらにそれぞれの動物の毛並みの違いを細かく表現しています。色のぬり方はカラーインクとパステルを使い，柔らかそうに，暖かそうに描くことを試みています。

Fur and Leather

In recent years the preservation of nature and protection of animals have become major social issues. As a result, few designers choose to use real animal fur in their designs. In accordance to such social movements, we are seing more and more imitation fur (fake fur) being used, a textile that used to be quite unpopular.

In recent years the quality of such imitation fur has been improving, so that designers are able to use both real and imitation fur according to their purpose. In addition, since imitation fur can be dyed in colors other than natural ones, and is less expensive than real fur, it is being used with less resistance in recent times.

We have selected designs here that may be used with real or imitation fur. We have also expressed in detail the difference in each animal's lie of hair. We have chosen colored inks and pastels to color the fur, conveying a sense of warmth and softness.

Color pencil, Color ink, Pastel, Hahnemühle paper

39

Color pencil, Color ink, Pastel, Hahnemühle paper

Color pencil, Color ink, Pastel, Hahnemühle paper

毛皮の描き方
Drawing Fur

①線画を描く。①Draw the line drawing.

②カラーインクをぬった後，②Draw in the lie of hair
　毛並みを描く。　　　　after applying colored
　　　　　　　　　　　　ink.

③パステルと柔らかめの色鉛筆で，毛並みを描く。

③Draw the lie of hair using pastels and soft colored pencils.

④顔，靴，靴下に色をつけ，全体に陰影をつけ完成。

④Apply color to the face, shoes, and socks. Complete by adding shadows.

毛皮の種類
Type of Fur

ミンク

毛並みが短く，はぎめの
うねりがある。

Mink

The hair is short, and
the seams are
winding.

カルガン・ラム

毛並みがチリチリとカー
ルしている。

Kalgan Lamb

The hair is short and
curly.

ムトン
毛並みが短く硬い。

Sheep Skin
The hair is short and
coarse.

フォックス
毛並みが長くて柔らかく，
ふあふあしている。

Fox
The hair is long, soft,
and fluffy.

着色の仕方
Applying Color

Color pencil, Color ink, Pastel, Hahnemühle paper

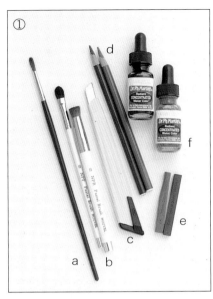

①必要な道具
　a 筆　　　　d 色鉛筆
　b パステル筆　e パステル
　c ナイフ　　　f カラーインク

④粉にしたパステルを，パステル筆につけ，全体に万遍なくぬる。

①Necessary equipment
　a. Brush　　　d. Colored pencils
　b. Pastel brush　e. Pastels
　c. Knife　　　　f. Colored ink

④Apply the powdered pastels to a pastel brush, uniformly applying the powder to the entire illustration.

②カラーインクを混ぜあわせ，希望の色をだし，カラーインクを全体にぬる。

⑤色鉛筆で毛並みをつける。細かく描けば描くほど，自然の感じに近くなる。

②Combine the colored inks to create the desired color, and apply to the entire illustration.

⑤Draw the lie of hair with colored pencils. The more detailed the hair is drawn, the more realistic and natural it will look.

③パステルをナイフで削り，粉にする。なるべく細かく削ること。数色を混ぜあわせ，希望の色にする。

⑥顔のメーキャップ，陰影など，残りの部分を仕上げ，最後にパステルが落ちないように，フキサチーフを全体に吹きつける。

③Shave the pastels with a knife, creating a powder. The powder should be as fine as possible. Combine several colors to create the desired color.

⑥Complete the make-up, shadows, and other details. Spray a fixative at the end so that the pastels do not come off.

パステルの粉があちこち散らないようにすること，また，強くこすり過ぎると紙がぼろぼろになるので注意すること。パステルは，べったりぬりたい時は指先を使い，軽くぬりたい時は筆を使うとよい。

Make sure that the pastel powder does not fly about. Do not rub the paper too strongly, since it will tear. When you wish to apply a thick coat of pastels, use your fingers, and a brush when a lighter coat is desired.

Color pencil, Color ink, Pastel, Hahnemühle paper

Color pencil, Color ink, Pastel, Hahnemühle paper

Color pencil, Color ink, Pastel, Hahnemühle paper

革

毛皮と同様に，最近では革もファッション企画に多く使
われています。革だけを使ったもの，革と布もしくはニ
ットを組合せたものなど，革の使われ方もさまざまです。
ブランドのイメージや企画のテーマに合わせ，いろいろ
なデザインが考えられます。色も毛皮と同じように，希
望の色に染めることができます。しかし，革は布と異な
り，大きさがまちまちです。牛皮のように大きいものも
あれば，爬虫類のように小さなものもあります。また，
同じ動物の革でも大小があります。そこで，デザインす
る時は，はぎめの位置をよく考え，革を無駄なく使うよ
うに心がける必要があります。ここではカラーインクと
パステルを用い，暖かそうに見える裏皮と，冷たく硬そ
うに見える表皮の描き方を紹介しています。

Leather

As with fur, leather is often used today in fashion designs.
Leather may be used alone, or combined with cloth or knits.
Many designs are possible to match the brand's image or the
theme of the line. Leather may be dyed in many colors, as with
fur. Unlike fabric, however, leather comes in uneven sizes and
shapes. There are large pieces, such as cow hide, and small
pieces from reptiles. In addition, sizes may be different even if
the same animal is chosen. Therefore, when designing a
garment made of leather, it is necessary to pay attention to the
location of seams, trying to waste the leather as little as possible. Using colored ink and pastels, we have introduced here
inside leather that appears warm, and the outer leather cold
and hard.

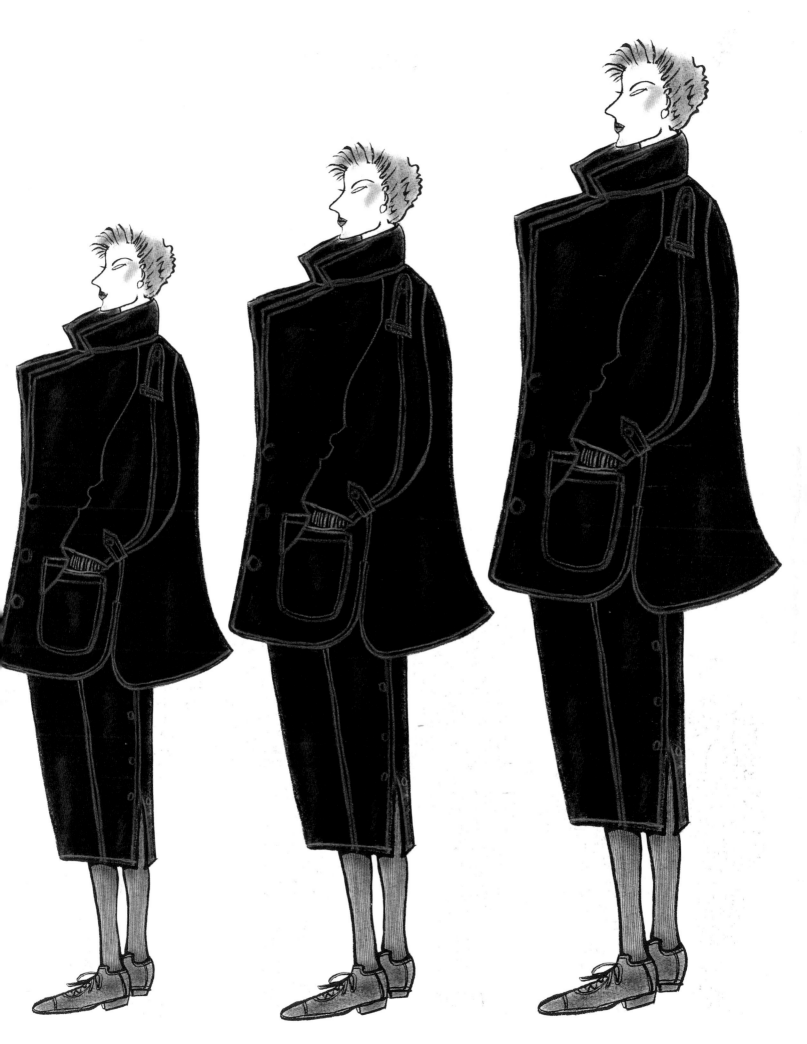

Color ink, Pastel, Hahnemühle paper

53

革とニットの組合わせ
Combination of leather and knits

Color ink, Pastel, Hahnemühle paper

Color ink, Pastel, Hahnemühle paper

靴下

最近では，店頭にいろいろ工夫された楽しく，魅力的な
靴下をよく見かけます。消費者は足元のおしゃれにも気
をくばるようになっています。

ファッションの企画も服をつくるというだけではなく，
頭の先から足の先までトータルで企画を考える時代にな
ってきています。特にカジュアルなブランドでは，靴下
の企画もトータルファッションの中で力をぬくことので
きないアイテムのひとつになっています。ブランドのコ
ンセプトやシーズンのテーマに合わせたデザインが考え
られます。ここではカジュアルで，大胆な模様の靴下を
いくつか紹介します。

Socks

Many fashionable and creative socks can be found in
shops today. Consumers are beginning to pay more
attention to their feet now.

We have entered an era in which fashion plans must
consider the total image, from head to toes, rather than
just the design of clothes. This is especially the case
with casual brands, which must consider socks as an
important item of the total fashion plan. Designs may
be considered according to the brand's concept or
season's theme. We have introduced here several
pairs of casual socks, with bold patterns.

Gouache, Pastel, Hahnemühle paper

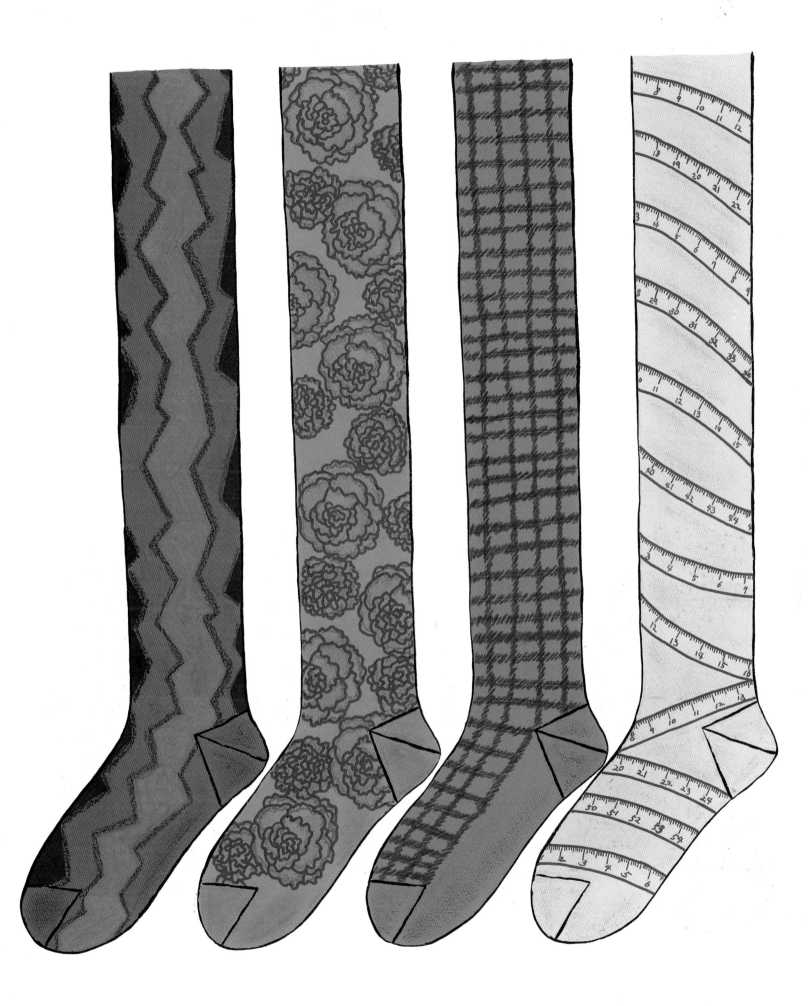

Gouache, Pastel, Hahnemühle paper

57

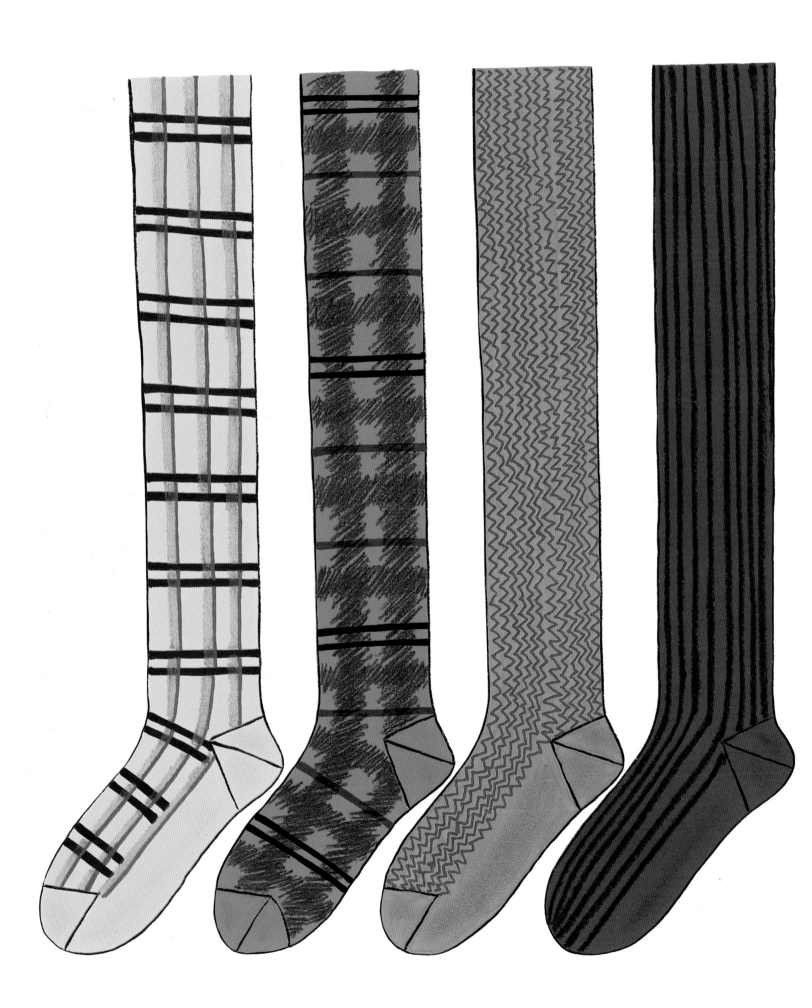

Gouache, Pastel, Hahnemühle paper

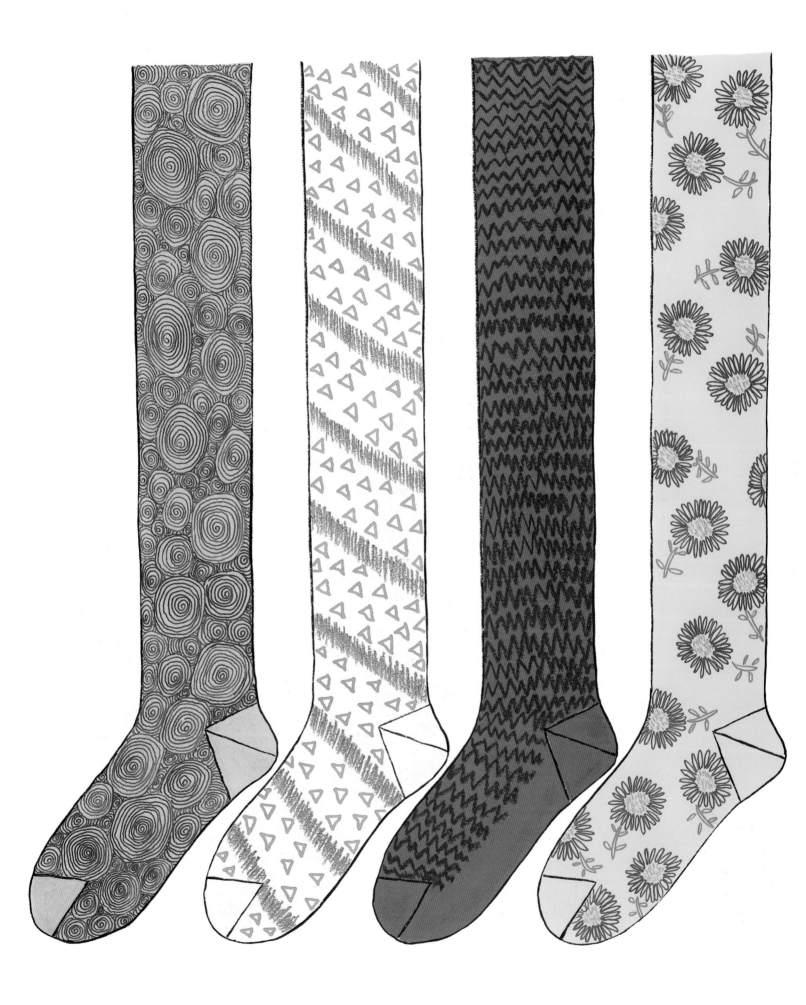

Gouache, Pastel, Hahnemühle paper

ニット

ニットはファッション企画にかかせないアイテムのひとつです。ニットは糸の太さや編方に左右されるため，それらの違いがよくわかるように注意して，ファッション画を描きます。ここではそれぞれの表現方法を紹介しながら，ニットの知識が得られるようにしています。

ニットは，裁断し縫製するカット・アンド・ソーやハイゲージと，1本の糸より染めて編む，手編，家庭機編，機械編，インターシャに大きく分けられます。カット・アンド・ソーは布とデザインの表現があまり変わらないので省略し，1本の糸より編むものをつぎに説明します。

ハイゲージ　　　細い糸で編むため編地は細い。裁断し縫製するため，布に近いデザインができる。あまりニット的な表現をしない方がよい。

手　　編　　　糸の太さによって違うが，いろいろ手のこんだ編地ができる。ざっくりとした感じやふわりとした柔らかな感じを表現することが大切。

家庭機編・機械編　　中細の糸で編まれたもの。ニットらしく表現するが，あまりざっくり重そうに表現しない。

インターシャ　　編地ではなく，ダイヤ柄など幾何学模様を大胆に工夫して表現する。

Knits

It is impossible to design a fashion plan without considering knits. Since knits vary greatly depending on the thickness of yarn or the type of knitting, it is important to draw the fashion illustrations showing these differences. We have introduced the different methods of expression here, explaining at the same time some facts about knits.

Knits may be divided into fabric that is cut and sewn, such as the "cut-and-sew" or high guage types, or those in which the yarn is dyed and then knit by hand, consumer or industrial knitting machines, as well as intarsia. Since the "cut-and-sew" types differ little in textile and design, we will not discuss them here. The following are the types knit from yarn, and not cut.

High Guage
Since thin yarn is used to knit the fabric, the material is thin. The resulting design is close to other cloth, since it is cut and sewn. It is best not to use a very knit-like expression.

Hand Knitting
Complex fabrics may be created, depending on the thickness of yarn.
It is important to convey baggy and soft expressions.

Knitting Machines
Medium-fine yarn was used to knit this. Although the knit texture should be expressed, it should not appear to be too heavy.

Intarsia
Boldly express the geometric patterns, such as diamonds, rather than a simple knit surface.

Gouache, Pastel, Hahnemühle paper

手編

手編とは編棒を用いて手で編むものをいいます。
基本的なものとして，棒針編，かぎ針編，アフガ
ン編があります。ここでは棒針を用いて手で編ん
だものといくつかの編地を紹介しています。

Gouache, Pastel, Hahnemühle paper

Hand Knitting

Hand knitting refers to the knitting method using needles.
The basic types are standard needle knitting, crocheting, and afghans. We have introduced several samples here of the standard needle knitting method.

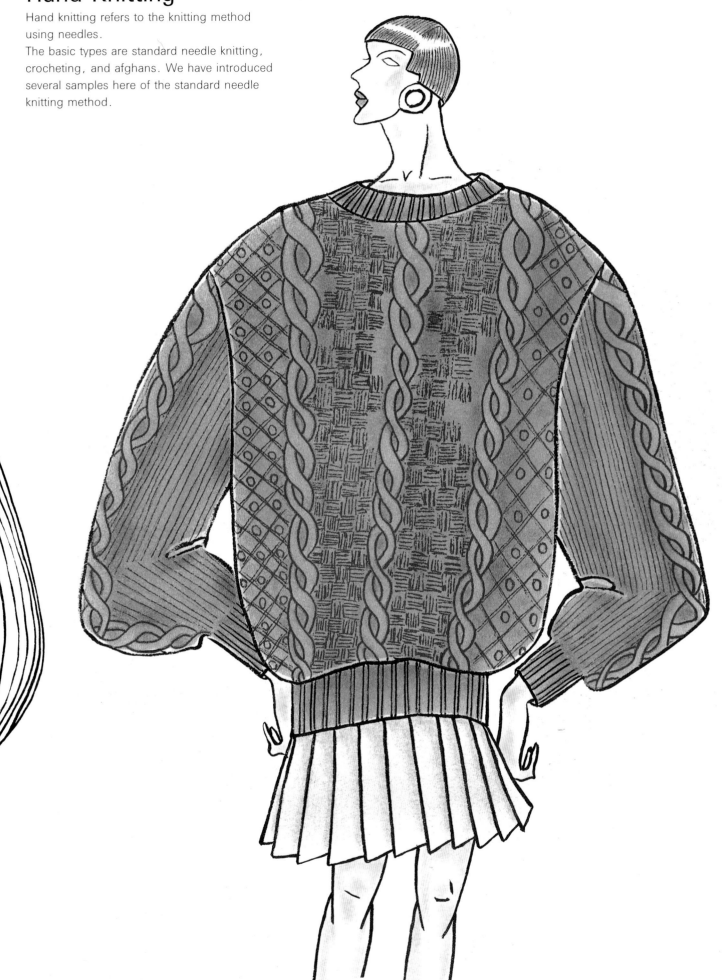

Gouache, Pastel, Hahnemühle paper

ニットの編地の描き方
Drawing Knit Textures

このセーターは右にある様々な編地を表現しています。
This sweater expresses the many textures to the right.

地柄と玉編
Texture and Ball Knit

1目ゴム編（リブ編）
1×1 Rib knit

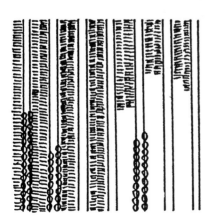

2目ゴム編（リブ編）
2×2 Rib knit

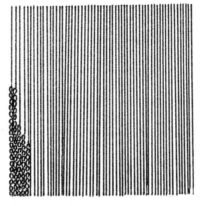

表編
Knit stitch

裏編
Purl stitch

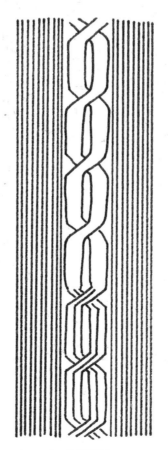

ケーブル編（縄編）
Cable knit

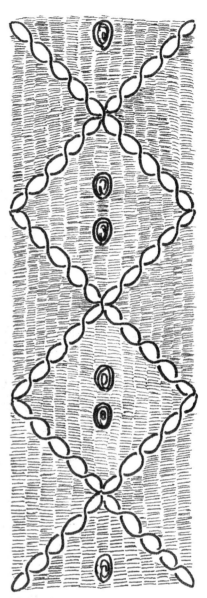

ケーブル編（縄編）と玉編
Cable knit and ball knit

鹿の子編
Dapple knit

65

Gouache, Pastel, Hahnemühle paper

ミドルゲージ

中細の糸を用いて，工業用編機や
家庭用編機で編んだもの。

Middle guage

Examples using a medium-fine
yarn, using consumer and
industrial knitting machines.

インターシャ

地糸による編地の中に数色の染糸を
用いて，柄模様を編みこんだもの。

Intarsia

Several different colors were used
to weave a design into the base
knit.

Gouache, Pastel, Hahnemühle paper

ハイゲージ

細い糸で編んだもの。
カット・アンド・ソーと同じように
型紙にもとづいて裁断縫製する。

High gauge

Knit with fine yarn.
As with "cut-and-sew" (sewing), a
pattern was used to cut and sew
the knit fabric.

Gouache, Pastel, Hahnemühle paper

インナー

現代のファッションではインナーが重要な位置をしめています。インナーとは，アウターに対する言葉です。タウンウエアのように，外で着るものをアウターといい，家の中で着たり，下着のように服の下に着るものをインナーといいます。ところが最近は，インナーとアウターの区別がうすれる傾向がみられます。若い歌手のステージを思い浮かべて下さい。インナーもデザイナーの活躍できる世界なのです。ここではインナーのアイテムとして，スポーツシャツ，パジャマ，ガウン，下着をデザインしています。それに〈着色の仕方〉として，ぼかし網を使って，細かい絵具のつぶを落すテクニックを紹介します。

Inner Wear

Inner clothes play an important role in today's fashion world. "Inner wear" is used in reference to "outer wear." "Outer wear" refers to clothes worn out of the house, and "inner wear" to those worn either inside the house, or under other clothing. However, in recent times it has become difficult to distinguish between these two. Think of concerts held by young singers. Designers can have a great influence now on inner wear, as well. We have selected here sports shirts, pyjamas, dressing gown, and underwear as examples of inner wear. We will also introduce the technique of using a shading net to apply color with small drops of paint.

Gouache, Color pencil, BFK Rives paper

Gouache, Color pencil, BFK Rives paper

Gouache, Color pencil, BFK Rives paper

着色の仕方
Appliying Color

絵具の濃さに注意することと，硬めの歯ブラシ（刷毛）を使うことがうまくできる秘訣です。
It is important to pay attention to the thickness of paint, and make sure to use a hard toothbrush (paint brush).

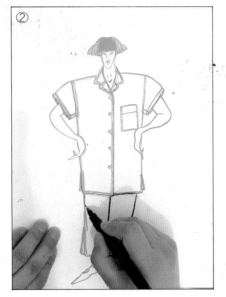

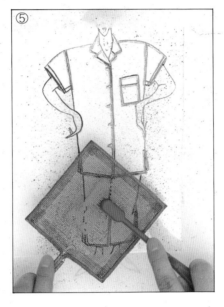

①必要な道具

　a 透明フィルム　　e 刷毛
　b 細いフェルトペン　f 歯ブラシ
　c カッターナイフ　　g 筆
　d ぼかし網　　　　　h 絵具

④ファッション画と切り抜いた透明
　フィルム。

②ファッション画の上に透明フィル
　ムを置き，フェルトペンで着色す
　る所を描く。この時，線より少し
　内側を描く。

⑤周辺を汚さないように紙でおおう。
　絵具をつけた歯ブラシ（刷毛）を，
　ぼかし網にこすりつけ，細かい絵
　具のつぶを落とす。

③線に沿って，透明フィルムをカッ
　ターで切り抜く。

⑥着色の終ったファッション画。こ
　れに色鉛筆とパステルではだ色を
　つけ，顔にメーキャップをし，靴や
　ボタンにも色をつけ，全体に陰影
　を与えると完成。

①Necessary Equipment

　a. Transparent film
　b. Fine felt-tipped pen
　c. Cutting knife
　d. Shading net
　e. Paint brush
　f. Toothbrush
　g. Brush
　h. Paint

④Illustration and cut out transpar-
　ent film.

②Place the transparent film over
　the illustration and use a felt-
　tipped pen to indicate where
　color is to be added.
　This should be done slightly
　inside the outline.

⑤Cover with paper so as not to dirty
　the surrounding area. Apply paint
　to the toothbrush (paint brush)
　and rub it across the shading net,
　dropping small drops of paint.

③Use a knife to cut the transparent
　film along the lines.

⑥Colored illustration. Color the
　skin with a colored pencil or pas-
　tel, apply make-up to the face,
　color the shoes and buttons, and
　finish the illustration by adding
　shadows.

Gouache, Color pencil, BFK Rives paper

Gouache, Color pencil, BFK Rives paper

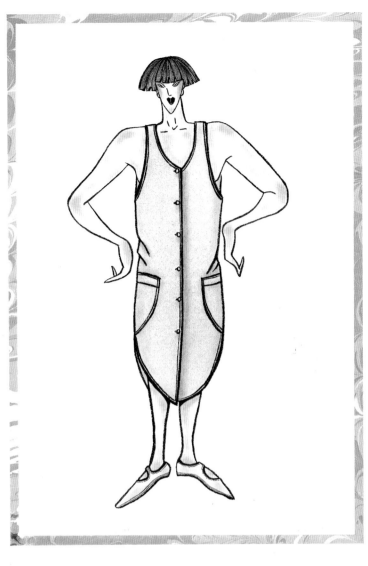

Gouache, Color pencil, BFK Rives paper

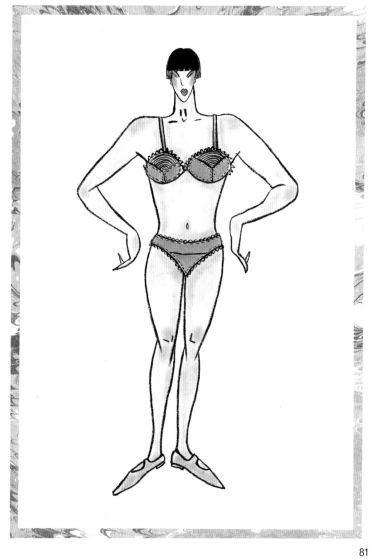

Gouache, Color pencil, BFK Rives paper

Gouache, Color pencil, BFK Rives paper

Gouache, Color pencil, BFK Rives paper

アウター

アウターとはインナーに対しての言葉です。

家の中で着るインナーに対して，家の外で着るものをアウターとかタウンウエアと呼びます。

アウターはファッション産業の中心であり，特に女性のアウターは，ファッションデザインの華といえるでしょう。さまざまなターゲット，さまざまなアイテムがあるので，それらをよく理解し，デザインすることがもっとも大切です。

ここではデザインをするためのイメージの作り方とマーカーの使い方を説明しています。

生活の中で目にふれたもの，耳に聞こえたものなどをどのようにデザインしたらよいか，デザインのもととなった具体的な写真も紹介しています。そこから得たイメージが服として表現されています。

着色にはマーカーを使っています。マーカーを使うと，水などいらないため，簡単に手早く描き上げることができます。このように便利なこともあって，最近ではマーカーがもっとも多く使われています。ところで，布には布目（地の目）があります。マーカーは比較的むらになりやすいので，布目に合わせて色をぬることが大切です。縦や横，斜めなどさまざまな方向からぬると，ぬり終えた時，あまりきれいではありません。布目に合わせるように一方向からぬると，多少むらになってもあまり気になりません。

Outer Wear

"Outer wear" is a term used as opposed to "inner wear". Inner wear is worn inside the house, and clothes worn out of the house are referred to either as outer wear or town wear.

Outer wear makes up the core of the fashion industry. Women's outer wear especially adds color to fashion designs. It is important to design the clothes with the specific target in mind, using the many available items. We have explained here the methods of creating images, and using markers. We have also introduced concrete photographs used as the basis for designs, showing how to design clothes using actual things touched and heard in our daily lives. Such images are expressed as finished designs.

We have used markers to apply color. Markers are suitable for quickly finishing the design, since water is unnecessary. Because of this convenience, markers are most commonly used today. Remember, however, that there is texture to fabric, and that it is important to apply color accordingly. It is difficult to evenly apply the color with markers. The result becomes unattractive when the marker is used in a combination of vertical, horizontal, and diagonal directions. If color is applied in accordance with the grain of fabric, a little unevenness will not be so noticeable.

マーカーの着色の仕方
（白残しぬり）

Applying Color with Markers
(Leaving Some White)

チューブの
イメージよりデザイン

Designed from the image of a tube

Marker, Bresdin Japon paper

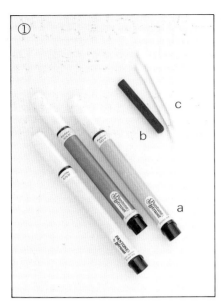

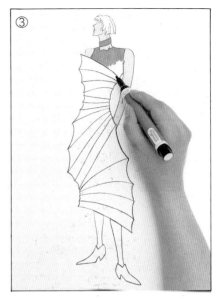

①必要な道具
　a マーカー
　　（肌，グレー，黄緑の３色）
　b パステル
　c 綿棒

②顔，手に肌色をぬる。目の部分は
　ぬらないこと。
④身ごろに黄緑色をぬる。光のあた
　っている部分はぬらないで，白く
　残す。

③インナーにグレー色をぬる。

⑤影になる部分に同色で，２度ぬり，
　３度ぬりをする。
⑥靴，靴下，髪の毛などに色をつけ，
　顔にメイクをすると完成。

①Necessary Equipment
　a. Markers
　(skin-tone, gray, and light
　green)
　b. Pastels
　c. Cotton applicator

②Apply the skin-tone to the face
　and hands. Do not color the
　eyes.

④Use the light green to color the
　body of the suit. Do not color
　the areas where light is hitting.
　Leave them white.

③Color the inner wear with the
　gray marker.

⑤Use the same color, applying it
　two or three times, to the
　shaded areas.

⑥Color the shoes, socks, hair,
　and apply make-up to complete
　the illustration.

マーカーを使う時は，線のぎりぎりまでぬると，線より
色がしみでるので，少し線の内側までぬるだけでよいで
す。線との間に少しぬり残しがあっても気にしなくてよ
いでしょう。

Since the color will spread a little, do not apply color
with markers up to the edge. Do not worry if there is
some white left between the color and lines.

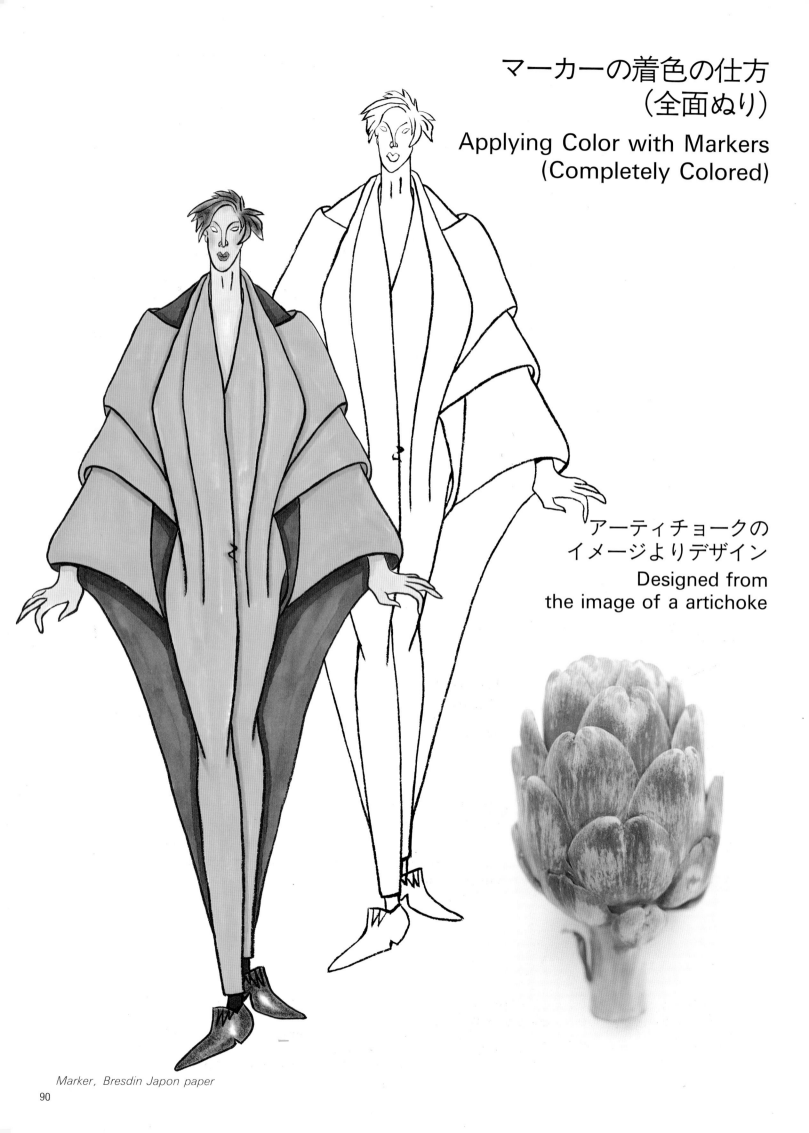

マーカーの着色の仕方
（全面ぬり）
Applying Color with Markers
(Completely Colored)

アーティチョークの
イメージよりデザイン
Designed from
the image of a artichoke

Marker, Bresdin Japon paper

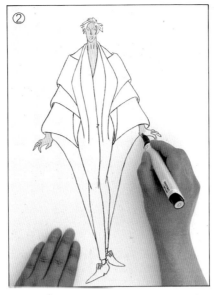
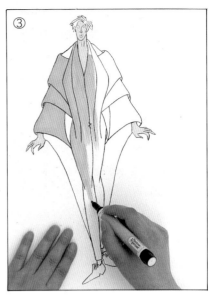

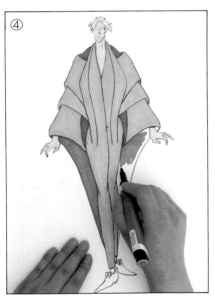
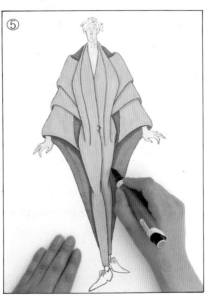
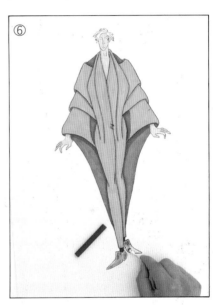

①色のグラデーション
　1度ぬり
　2度ぬり
　3度ぬり
④茶色をぬる。

①Color Gradation
　1 coat
　2 coats
　3 coats
④Apply the brown.

②顔，手などに肌色をぬる。目の部分はぬらないこと。

⑤同色を，2度，3度ぬり，陰影をつける。

②Apply the skin-tone to the face and hands. Do not color the eyes.

⑤Use the same color, applying it two or three times, to the shaded areas.

③身ごろの部分にオレンジ色をぬる。

⑥靴，靴下，髪の毛などに色をつけ，顔にメイクすると完成。

③Use the orange to color the body.

⑥Color the shoes, socks, hair, and apply make-up to complete the illustration.

同色のマーカーを，2度，3度重ねてぬるか，グレーの色をぬると陰影ができ，立体的に見えます。陰影をつける時は続けてぬらず，1度ぬったらしばらく時間をおいてぬると色が濃くなり，うまくゆきます。

Use the same colored marker to apply two or three coats, or a gray marker to add shadows, making the illustration appear three-dimensional. When adding shadows, wait until the ink is dry before applying the next coat. This makes the color darker and more realistic.

花のイメージよりデザイン

とがった形をした花, 丸い形をした花, 数枚
の花びらや多数の花びらが重なりあってでき
ている花など, さまざまな花のもっているイ
メージをデザインしています。

Marker, Bresdin Japon paper

Using Floral Images

The different images of flowers, those that are pointed, rounded, with few or many petals, are used in the designs.

Marker, Bresdin Japon paper

エアキャップの イメージよりデザイン

包装用のエアキャップは，規則正しくふくら んだ形が新しい素材を思わせます。薄い布の 中に入れる綿の量やステッチの模様によって， 素材の表情が変わってくるでしょう。

Marker, Bresdin Japon paper

Using Air-Cap Images

The air-cap packaging material has uniform, inflated shapes, giving it the image of a new material. By varying the amount of cotton in the thin cloth, and the design of the stitching, a variety of expressions may be achieved.

Marker, Bresdin Japon paper

Marker, Bresdin Japon paper

Using Origami (Folded Paper) Images

A single sheet of paper is given interesting three-dimensionality by folding it. Such images, of folds, concave and convex shapes, were used in this design.

Marker, Bresdin Japon paper

メンズ

ファッション画は，力強く描けば描くほど男性的に，やわらかくなめらかに描けば中性的で，女性的に見えます。ブランドのイメージによって異なりますが，一般的に，メンズのファッション画は男っぽく，がっしりとした感じに描くのが基本です。それには，線はなるべく直線的に，首は太く，肩幅は広く，ウエストはあまりくびれないように描きます。女性にくらべ，顔の表情には動きがあまりなくてよいでしょう。ただし，体のプロポーションは女性と変わりません。ブランドによっては，中性的なイメージに描く必要があるでしょう。

ここではいくつかのアイテムに分け，男性的なファッション画と，やや中性的なファッション画を紹介しています。メンズ独特のボリュウム感や表情が理解できるでしょう。

Men's Clothes

Powerful fashion illustrations appear masculine, and soft, smooth ones more neutral or feminine. Although each brand differs, it is most common to draw illustrations for men's designs with strong, bold lines, so that the figure appears masculine. The lines should be as straight as possible, with the neck thick, the shoulders broad, and the waist not too curved. The face should be less expressive than illustrations of women. However, the body's proportions are the same as a woman's. Some brands will require the figure to have a more unisex image.

We have divided the figures here according to item, introducing masculine and rather unisex fashion illustrations. You should be able to understand the expressions and boldness of the illustrations unique to men's fashion.

Gouache, Pastel, Hahnemühle paper

Gouache, Pastel, Hahnemühle paper

Gouache, Pastel, Hahnemühle paper

Gouache, Pastel, Hahnemühle paper

靴

靴は靴下と同様に，ファッション企画の中でかかせないもののひとつになっています。服のデザインイメージに合わせて靴のデザインも考え，トータルでひとつのブランドを着こなせるように企画をたてます。

靴のデザインは多くしません。1回のコレクションで3，4点といったところでしょう。靴をデザインする時のポイントは，デザインのみ優先させるのではなく，履きごこちを考えることです。どんなに形のよい靴でも，しばらく履いて足が痛くなっては，せっかくのおしゃれも台無しです。靴は服以上に履きごこちをたえず考える必要があります。ここでは，デザインぽいものからベーシックなものまで，色々なタイプの靴をいくつか紹介しています。

Gouache, Pastel, Hahnemühle paper

Shoes

As with socks, shoes are an essential item in a fashion plan. Shoes must be designed according to the design image of the clothes, so that consumers can wear the complete line.

Only a few shoe designs are used per collection, each using no more than three or four designs. It is important when designing shoes to remember that priority should be given to comfort, and not merely the design. No matter how excellent the design, if the person wearing the shoes is in pain, the efforts are wasted. It is more important to keep comfort in mind with shoes than it is with clothes. We have introduced a number of shoes here, some design-oriented, and others more basic.

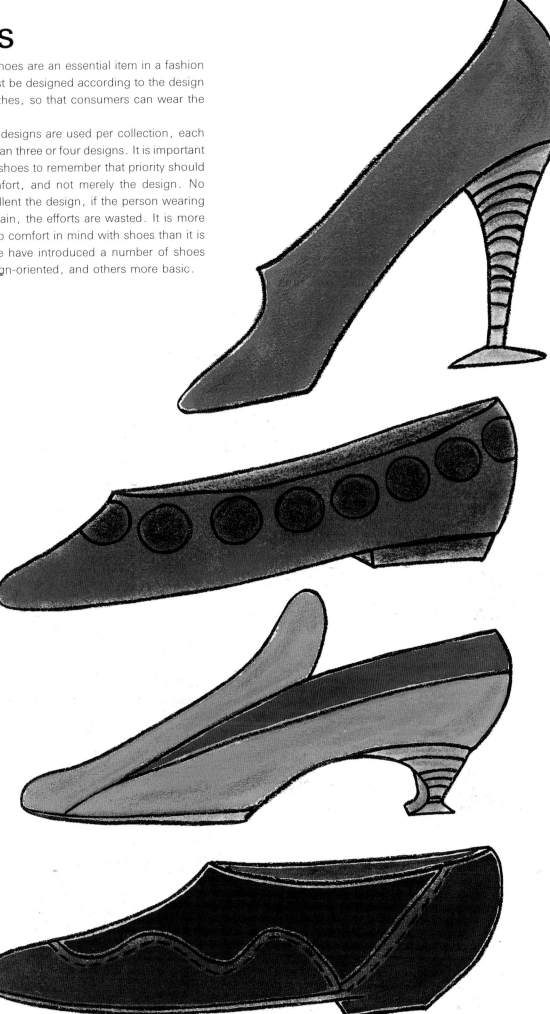

Gouache, Pastel, Hahnemühle paper

Gouache, Pastel, Hahnemühle paper

Gouache, Pastel, Hahnemühle paper

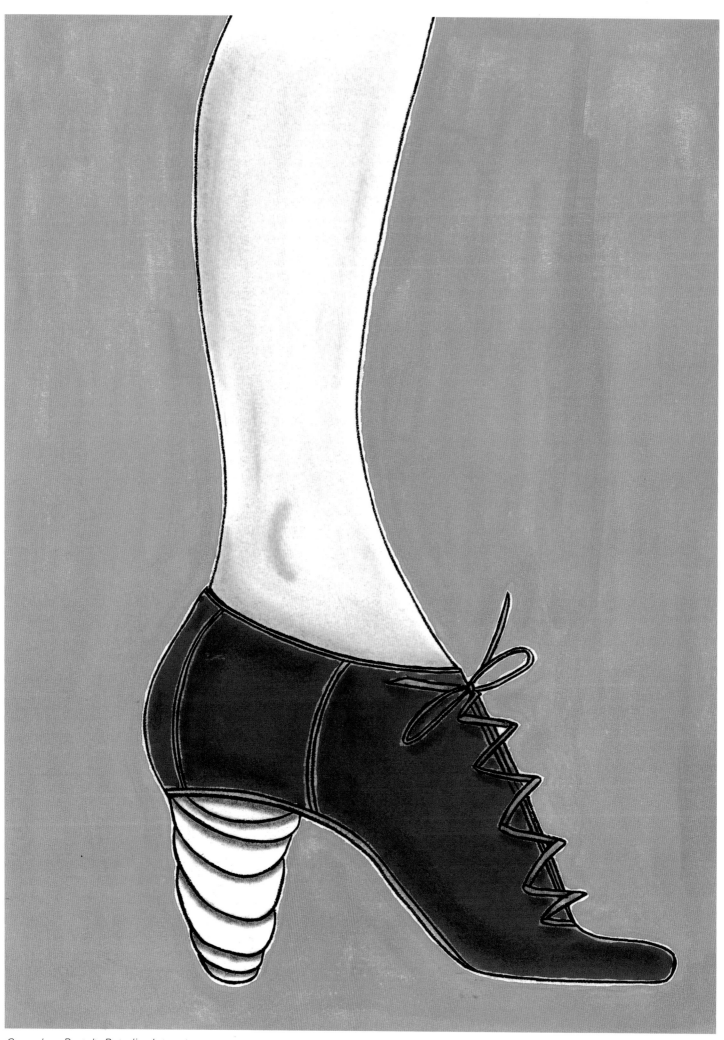

Gouache, Pastel, Bresdin Japon paper

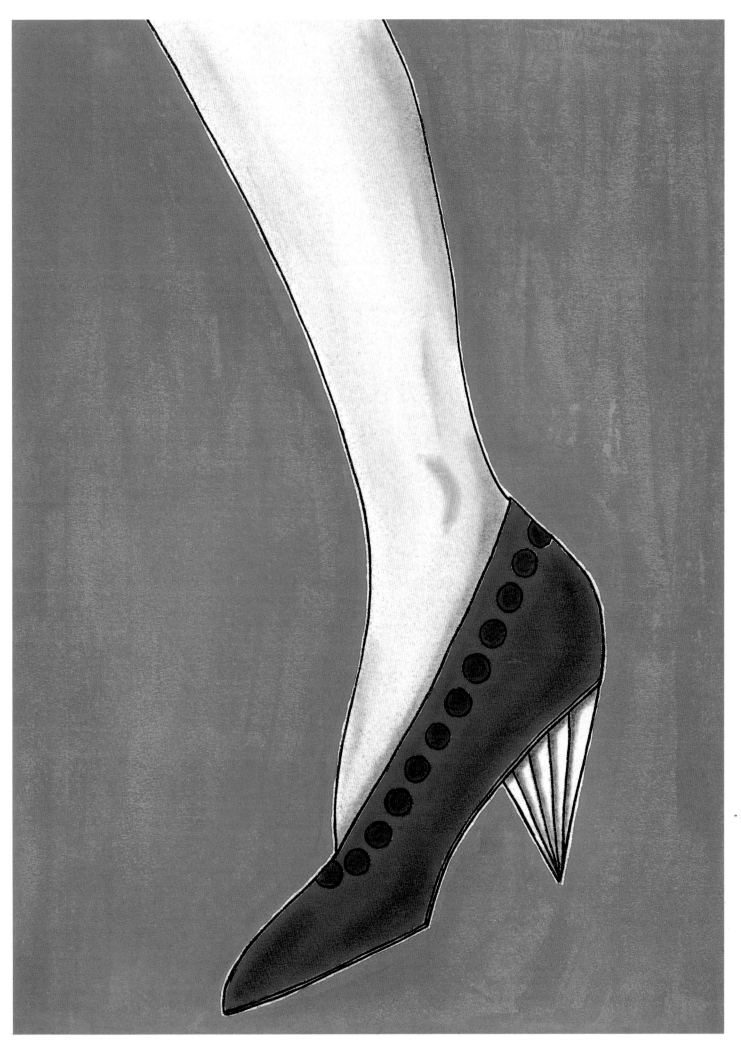

Gouache, Pastel, Bresdin Japon paper

帽子

最近はあまり帽子をかぶらなくなったため，ファッション企画に帽子のデザインを入れるブランドは少なくなっています。それでもブランドのイメージによっては，どうしても帽子の企画が必要になります。時には，流行に大きく左右され，帽子がアイテムとして重要視されることもあります。帽子の使い方は大きく分けて二通りあります。ひとつはライフスタイルにどうしても必要なもの，もうひとつはまったくおしゃれのためにかぶるもの。ここではおしゃれのためにかぶる，さまざまな形の帽子を描いています。

Hats

Since fewer people wear hats today, there are not many manufacturers including hats in their fashion plans. However, depending on the brand's image, it is sometimes necessary to design hats. In some cases we even find that, according to recent trends, hats are given great importance as an essential fashion item. There are two major ways of using hats. One is based on the person's life style, in which hats are essential. Other people choose to wear hats as a form of fashion. We have illustrated several of the latter type.

Gouache, Pastel, Hahnemühle paper

バッグ

現代のファッションはトータルで企画をたてるブランド
が多くなっています。バッグも忘れてはならない商品の
ひとつです。靴と同じように，量としては多くは作りま
せんが，1回のコレクションで2，3点は提案します。バ
ッグもシーズンのコンセプトに合わせてデザインします。

Bags

Many designer brands feature total fashion plans today.
Bags are important fashion items, as well. Although not
many are designed, as in the case with shoes, each
collection will suggest two or three designs. Bags
should be designed according to the season's concept.

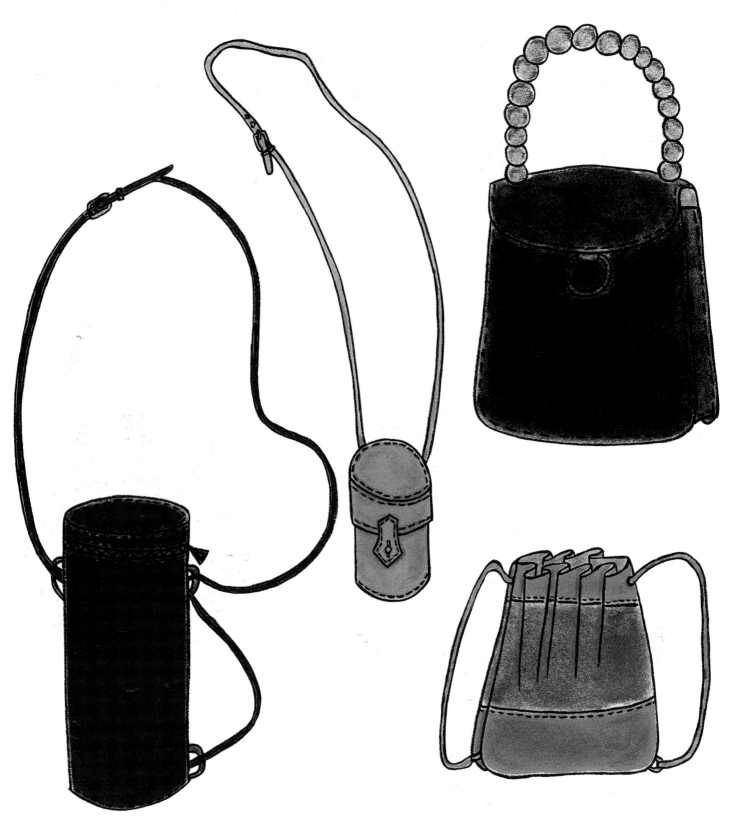

Gouache, Pastel, Hahnemühle paper

Gouache, Pastel, Hahnemühle paper

113

子供

ここ数年，子供服のブランドも増え，メーカーは子供服のブランドに力を入れています。それを証拠に，街のあちこちに子供服の新しい店ができているのを見かけます。ライバルが多くなった結果，子供服にも，より個性的で差別化した服作りが要求される時代になってきました。

子供は年齢によって大きさのバランスが違います。年齢が下がれば頭が大きく，ウエストや手足がふっくらとしています。大きくなるにしたがって，ウエストが細くなり全体にスマートになります。そこではじめに，年齢にそった成長の過程を線画で紹介してみました。

デザインも，大きくなるにしたがって，大人とあまり変わらなくなります。デザインする時は，何才くらいの子供の服をデザインするかよく考える必要があります。やさしく可愛らしく描くことがもっとも大切です。

Children's Clothes

We have seen an increase in children's designer brands in recent years. Accordingly, manufacturers are placing more emphasis on the development of these brands. As proof of this, there is an increasing number of children's clothes shops in the cities. As a result of the increase in the number of rivals, we have entered an era in which children's clothes are becoming more unique and individualistic.

Children must be drawn differently according to their age.

The younger the age, the bigger the head, and the rounder and softer the waist, arms, and legs. The waist becomes more narrow as the child grows older. We have introduced line drawings of children according to their age.

The design of clothes differs little from those for adults as the child matures. It is very important to keep in mind the child's age when designing the clothes. It is most important to draw cute, innocent-looking clothes.

Gouache, Pastel, Hahnemühle paper

Gouache, Pastel, Hahnemühle paper

Gouache, Pastel, Bresdin Japon paper

Gouache, Pastel, Bresdin Japon paper

Gouache, Pastel, Bresdin Japon paper

Gouache, Pastel, Bresdin Japon paper

Gouache, Pastel, Pastesdin Japon paper

Gouache, Pastel, Bresdin Japon paper

〈FASHION LOOK〉について

長いあいだ私は，ファッション画について不満を持っていました。デザイナー自身の描いたものは，製品化を目的とするあまり絵としての完成度に欠け，イラストレーターのものは，製品化を目的としないために服のデザインに劣ることが多いと思っていました。私はこの本の中で，両者の欠点を乗り越えようと試みました。それと同時に，服作りの現場では使い捨てになりがちなファッション画にもう少し注目してもらい，できれば絵画作品としても自立したファッション画を描こうと努めました。それはパリの学校でファッションやテキスタイルのデザインを学んだ時から，久しく考えていたことでもあります。このような絵を私は〈ファッションルック〉と呼び，描き続けています。

1点1点をていねいに描くからとはいえ，〈ファッションルック〉は服作りの知識に欠けがちなイラストレーターの描いたものとは違います。彼らの作品にはあいまいな線や余分なしわが多すぎ，ポーズにも動きがありすぎるため，服のデザインがよくわからないことがあります。これではパタンナーが，ファッション画から立体を想像し，パターンを作ろうとする時にとまどってしまうでしょう。〈ファッションルック〉は，デザイナーの意図がよくわかるように描いています。本書にあるファッション画から，パターンをおこすことは簡単なのではないでしょうか。

〈ファッションルック〉を描くこつは，服のデザインがよく見えるポーズを採用すること，しわを多く描かないこと，素材感やデザインの細かいところまで正確に描くこと，そして絵として魅力のあるファッション画に仕上げることなどです。例えば，何故しわを多く描かないのでしょうか。しわが多くなると，古着のようになってしまいます。ファッション画では，最初に袖をとおした時の，真新しい服に描く必要があります。

このような考えに基づき，実際のデザイン活動で描いたインナーや毛皮のファッション画をご覧になって頂こうと，1990年の秋，私は原宿の画廊で，「柳沢元子ファッションイラストレーション展」を催しました。その時に来廊された多くの人が，私の提唱するファッション画について興味を示してくださったのですが，とりわけ，グラフィック社のOさんには熱心に見て頂き，その結果がこのような本に結実しました。その展覧会に展示された27点の作品もこの本の中に収められています。

あらゆる分野が分業化する傾向にある現在，ファッションの世界もその例にもれません。しかし，ファッションデザイナーは自らの手で，白い紙にまだ見たことのない新しい服を描かなければなりません。何故なら，そこからファッションの創造がはじまるからです。このような時，〈ファッションルック〉という考え方が，ファッション画を描こうとする人のささやかな助けともなれば，デザイナーとして，またこの本の著者として，このうえない幸せです。

柳 沢 元 子

About *FASHION LOOK*

I have been unhappy with fashion illustrations for a long time. Those drawn by designers concentrate too much on selling the finished product, and are inferior as illustrations. The sketches by illustrators, however, do not place enough emphasis on the finished product, resulting in inferior designs. I have tried to overcome the weaknesses of both groups in this book. At the same time, I would like people to pay more attention to fashion illustrations, often thrown away after being used, and have tried to create illustrations that may be viewed as pieces of art. This is something I have been contemplating since studying fashion and textile design in Paris. I call these illustrations "Fashion Look," and have continued to draw them.

Although each illustration is drawn carefully, this does not mean that "Fashion Look" drawings are the same as sketches drawn by illustrators, who often do not have the basic knowledge of making clothes. Their illustrations have too many vague lines and wrinkles, the poses having too much action, making it difficult to comprehend the actual design.

This confuses the person making the pattern, who tries to look at the fashion illustration and create a three-dimensional image. "Fashion Look" illustrations are drawn so that the designer's intentions are easily understood. It should be a simple task to create patterns from the illustrations introduced in this book.

There are several points to remember when drawing "Fashion Look" illustrations: 1) choose a pose that enhances the design, 2) do not draw many wrinkles, 3) carefully draw the texture and details of the design, and 4) complete an illustration that has value as a piece of art. Taking one of these points as an example, there should be few wrinkles since the clothes look second-hand if there are too many.

It is necessary to draw the illustration showing the garment as it would look the first time it is worn.

In order for people to actually have a chance to see fashion illustrations of inner wear and fur items, I held an exhibition titled "Motoko Yanagisawa's Fashion Illustrations" in a gallery in Harajuku, Tokyo in the fall of 1990. Many people who visited the gallery showed interest in my form of fashion illustrations. Among them was Ms. Oe of Graphic-sha, who enthusiastically viewed my work. This encounter resulted in this publication. The 27 illustrations shown at the exhibition can be found in this book, as well.

As with other industries, labor is being divided in the world of fashion. However, fashion designers must draw an illustration of an unseen design on a piece of white paper with their own hands. This is because this is the beginning of the creation of fashion. As a designer and the author of this book, I hope that the concept of "Fashion Look" will be of use to you in such situations.

MOTOKO YANAGISAWA

著者紹介

柳沢 元子 (やなぎさわ もとこ)

大妻女子大学卒業。NHK 勤務後，渡仏。パリ国立美術学校(ボーザール)でデッサンとクロッキーを学ぶ。その後，パリ・エスモード学院 (ESMOD Paris) に入学し，ファッションデザイン科，及びテキスタイル科を同時に修了。卒業式の際に，著名デザイナー，ジャーナリストの審査の結果，《最優秀学生賞》(Le Prix du Meilleur Elève) を授賞。デザイナー，イラストレーターとして活躍後，帰国。

1982年より1986年迄，鐘紡株式会社ファッション事業部チーフデザイナー。

1984年，原宿に「柳沢デザイン事務所」を設立し，ファッションのデザインを主に，ブランド開発，テキスタイルデザイン，ファッションイラストレーション等の業務を行い，現在に至る。東京家政大学服飾美術学科等講師。

主な仕事：ムーンバット(株)毛皮及び革のデザイン。
　　　　　帝人(株)先物用コレクションのデザイン企画。
　　　　　(株)西武百貨店 リバテイのファッションデザインなど。

個　　　展：1990年9月 「柳沢元子ファッションイラストレーション展」(原宿，ギャラリー神宮苑)
　　　　　1990年12月 「柳沢元子ファッションイラストギャラリー」(船橋，西武百貨店)
　　　　　1991年10月 「柳沢元子ファッションイラストレーション展」(渋谷，電力館)

柳沢デザイン事務所
　　〒150 東京都渋谷区神宮前1-10-34-406
　　Phone 03-3408-6247

Profile

Motoko Yanagisawa

After graduating from the Otsuma Women's College, Ms. Yanagisawa worked for NHK Broadcasting before moving to France. She studied dessin and croquis (sketching) at the Paris National Academy of Art (Beaux Arts) before entering the Esmod Paris Academy, where she simultaneously completed the fashion design and textile curricula and was given the award of Excellence, "Le Prix du Meileur Elève".

Ms. Yanagisawa worked for Kanebo Co., Ltd. as chief designer of the fashion department. In 1984 she established the Yanagisawa Design studio in Harajuku, and has been working in the fields of brand development, textile design, and fashion illustration. She also teaches in Tokyo Kasei University's department of fashion and art.

Exhibitions:

September, 1990　Gallery Jingu-en, Harajuku
December, 1990　Seibu Department Store, Funabashi
October, 1991　Denryoku-kan, Shibuya

YANAGISAWA DESIGN STUDIO
　　1-10-34-406, JINGUMAE, SHIBUYA, TOKYO

ファッション ルック
〈ファッションデザイナーが描くモードイラストレーション〉

1992年3月25日　初版第1刷発行

著　者　柳沢元子 (やなぎさわもとこ) ©
発行者　久世　利郎

発行所　株式会社グラフィック社
　　　　〒102 東京都千代田区九段北1-9-12
　　　　☎03 (3263) 4318 振替・東京3-114345

印　刷　錦明印刷株式会社
製　本　大口製本株式会社
写　植　三和写真工芸株式会社
翻　訳　レスリー・ハリントン

落丁・乱丁本はお取替え致します。
本書の収録内容の無断転写，複写，引用等を禁じます。
Printed in Japan

ISBN4-7661-0671-7 C3071